MOUSE JOKE BOOK

FUNFAX™

A Funfax Book
First published in Great Britain in 1999 by Funfax Ltd.,
an imprint of Dorling Kindersley Limited,
9 Henrietta Street, London WC2E 8PS
Based on a book first published in 1990.
Funfax concept © Funfax Ltd
© Disney

LIBRARY OF LAUGHS

Dentistry by Phil Macavity

Wedding Memories by Ann E. Versary

Teatime by Roland Butter

The Stupid Striker by Mr Goal

Tape Recorders by Cass Ette

Waterproof Clothes by Anne O'Rack

Old Furniture by Anne Teak

Splash! by Eileen Dover

Love Your Microwave by Andy Gadget

Falling by Mr Step

Cross the Road by Luke Bothways

Au Revoir by C. U. Later

Call For Help by Linda Hand

The Winner by Vic Torious

Bellringing For Beginners by Paula Rope

Bricks and Mortar by Bill Ding

MICKEY MOUSE
JOKE BOOK

MUSICAL MADNESS

Teacher: Why did Tchaikovsky write this piece in four flats?
Pupil: He had to move house three times while he was composing it.

Tuner: I've come to tune your piano.
Mr Smith: But I didn't send for you.
Tuner: No, but your neighbours did.

What's the best birthday present for a little boy?
A drum takes a lot of beating.

What musical instrument did the ancient Britons play?
The Anglo Saxonphone.

What's musical and very useful in a supermarket?
A Chopin Liszt.

What comes before a tuba?
A one-ba.

What fish is musical?
A piano tuna.

Did you hear about the girl who put her radio in the fridge?
She wanted to listen to some cool music.

What is Dracula's favourite song?
Fangs for the Memory.

KNOCK, KNOCK!

Knock, knock!
Who's there?
Tamara.
Tamara who?
Tamara is another day.

Knock, knock!
Who's there?
Major.
Major who?
Major open the door.

Knock, knock!
Who's there?
Cows go.
Cows go who?
No, owls go who,
cows go moo!

Knock, knock!
Who's there?
Hatch.
Hatch who?
That's a nasty
cold you've got.

Knock, knock!
Who's there?
Juno.
Juno who?
Juno what time it is?

Knock, knock!
Who's there?
Roland.
Roland who?
Roland butter, please.

Knock, knock!
Who's there?
Carmen.
Carmen who?
Carmen get me!

Knock, knock!
Who's there?
Tish.
Tish who?
Bless you!

Knock, knock!
Who's there?
Pudding.
Pudding who?
Pudding your shoes
on before your
trousers is a bad idea.

Knock, knock!
Who's there?
Cook.
Cook who?
Stop doing bird
impressions and
let me in.

Knock, knock!
Who's there?
Honeydew.
Honeydew who?
Honeydew you want
to go out tonight?

Knock, knock!
Who's there?
Ida.
Ida who?
Ida terrible time
getting here!

© Disney

CROSS BREEDS

What do you get if you cross a jelly with a tall building in Paris?
The Trifle Tower.

What do you get if you cross a snowball with a shark?
Frostbite.

What do you get if you cross a prehistoric monster with a sleeper?
A dinosnore.

What do you get if you cross a sheep with a radiator?
Central bleating.

What do you get if you cross a lawn with a kangaroo?
A grasshopper.

What do you get if you cross a frog with a flower?
A croakus.

What do you get if you cross a biscuit with
a hammer?
Crumbs.

What do you get if you cross a big dog with
an oak?
A tree with a very loud bark.

What do you get if you cross music with
an insect?
Humbug.

What do you get if you cross elves with
a sponge mixture?
Fairy cakes.

SPORTING NONSENSE

If there's a referee in football and an umpire in cricket, what is there in bowls?
Goldfish.

What is a kangaroo's favourite sport?
The long jump.

In what game do players have to carry a pig?
Backgammon.

What do martial arts fighters like to eat?
Karate chops.

What does the winner lose in a race?
His breath.

MICKEY MOUSE
JOKE BOOK

What does a bee wear when it goes jogging?
A swarm-up suit.

Why were the spiders playing football in a saucer?
They were practising for the cup.

What does a swimmer wear to work?
A bathing suit.

Why did the chicken run on to the football pitch?
Because the referee whistled for a fowl.

Why are lawyers good basketball players?
They spend a lot of time in court.

© Disney

9

DID YOU HEAR...?

Did you hear about the little boy who was named after his father?
They called him Dad.

Did you hear about the two eggs in a saucepan?
One said, "Gosh it's hot in here!" The other one said, "This is nothing. Wait until you get out, you'll really crack up!"

Did you hear about the banker who got bored with his job?
He lost interest.

Did you hear about the man with a seagull on his head?
He was called Cliff.

Did you hear about the two red blood cells?
They loved in vein.

Did you hear about the angry refrigerator?
It lost its cool.

Did you hear about the man who bought
a paper shop?
It blew away.

Did you hear about the world's worst athlete?
He ran a bath and came second.

Did you hear about the two acrobats who
got married?
They were head over heels in love.

Did you hear about the thumb that kissed
the finger?
They were in glove.

ANIMAL ANTICS

What do you call a skunk that's disappeared forever? Ex-stinked.

What's a pig's favourite ballet? Swine Lake.

Why do cows wear bells? Because their horns don't work.

What animals use nutcrackers? Toothless squirrels.

What's a hedgehog's favourite food? Prickled onions.

What creatures didn't go into
Noah's Ark in pairs?
Maggots – they went in apples.

What do animals
in zoos read?
Gnus papers.

What does a bird use for
an emergency landing?
His sparrowchute.

Why does a lion have a fur coat?
Because it would look silly in a
plastic mac.

Where do sheep get
their hair cut?
At the baa-baas shop.

SCHOOLTIME TICKLERS

MICKEY MOUSE
JOKE BOOK

"It's time to get up. You've got to go to school."
"I don't want to. All the teachers hate me
and the pupils despise me. Give me one
good reason."
"You're the headmaster!"

Why is the school football pitch always so soggy?
Because the players are always dribbling.

Teacher: If I had fifty apples in one hand and
thirty apples in the other, what would I have?
Pupil: Big hands!

Teacher: Can you make a sentence with the
word fascinate in it?
Pupil: My dad has nine buttons on his waistcoat
but he can only fascinate.

Son: I'm too tired to do my homework.
Mother: Don't be silly – hard work has never killed anyone yet.
Son: Then why should I risk being the first!

Why did the cyclops close his school?
Because he only had one pupil.

Pupil: I is...
Teacher: Where's your grammar?
You must say "I am".
Pupil: Okay. I am the ninth letter of the alphabet.

Teacher: Where are the Andes?
Pupil: At the end of the armies.

HYSTERICAL HISTORY

Teacher: Can you name the Tudor monarchs?
Pupil: Henry VII, Henry VIII, Edward VI,
Mary, er...
Teacher: Who came after Mary?
Pupil: Was it her little lamb?

Which English king had a heart transplant?
Richard the Lionheart.

What did one historian say to the other
historian?
Let's talk about old times.

Which Scottish king fell over all the time?
Robert the Bruise.

Teacher: What was the first thing Elizabeth I did
when she came to the throne?
Pupil: She sat down.

MICKEY MOUSE
JOKE BOOK

© Disney

How did the early explorers travel to America?
By Colum-bus.

King Arthur: How much do your rooms cost?
Innkeeper: Thirty pounds a knight.

How do we know that Christopher Columbus
was economical?
Because he went thousands of miles on one
galleon.

What was Sir Lancelot's favourite game?
Knights and crosses.

Who invented the steam engine?
Watt's-his-name.

TRAVELLERS' TALES

Sam: When we were at the seaside a crab bit one of my dad's toes.
Pam: Which one?
Sam: I don't know – all crabs look the same to me.

Passenger: I've never flown before. The pilot will bring us down safely, won't he?
Air hostess: Of course he will, madam – he's never left anyone up there yet.

What will they do when the Forth Bridge collapses?
Build a fifth.

Dan: Once I was shipwrecked and lived on a tin of sardines for a whole week.
Stan: I'm surprised you didn't fall off!

Mr and Mrs Brown were off on their holiday. Arriving at the airport, Mr Brown said, "I wish I'd brought the piano." "Whatever for?" asked Mrs Brown. "Because I've left the tickets on it!"

MICKEY MOUSE JOKE BOOK

Jo: My wife's gone to the West Indies.
Mo: Jamaica?
Jo: No, she wanted to go.

Where do bunny pilots learn to fly?
In the Hare Force.

Where do bees wait for transport?
At a buzz stop.

What do you get if you cross a frog with a 747?
A plane that makes short hops.

Where do travelling cows disappear mysteriously?
In the Bermooda Triangle.

HORSE LAUGHS

The thunder god went for a ride on his favourite horse. "I'm Thor!" he cried. The horse replied, "You forgot your thaddle, thilly!"

Why did the foal suck a throat sweet?
Because he was a little horse.

How do you hire a horse?
Put a brick under each foot.

Where do you take a sick horse?
To horsepital.

Why did the farmer call his horse Blacksmith?
Because the horse kept making a bolt for the door.

FROGGY FUN

What do you call a frog spy?
A croak and dagger agent.

What happens when a frog breaks down?
He gets toad away.

What's a frog's favourite sweet?
A lollihop.

What goes Croak! Croak! when it's misty?
A froghorn.

What's green and goes dah-dit, dah-dah, dah-dit?
Morse toad.

What's a frog's favourite drink?
Croak.

What's green on the inside, white on the outside and hops?
A frog sandwich.

JUNGLE JAPES

What do you call a bad-tempered gorilla?
Sir.

What do you do if you find a gorilla sleeping in your bed?
Sleep somewhere else.

What's black and white and very noisy?
A zebra with a drum kit.

What goes round the jungle grunting and sending other animals to sleep?
A wild bore.

What card game do crocodiles like best?
Snap.

MICKEY MOUSE JOKE BOOK

How do you stop a skunk from smelling?
Put a peg on its nose.

Who's purple and swings through the trees?
Tarzan of the Grapes.

What does Tarzan sing at Christmas?
"Jungle bells, jungle bells, jungle all the way!"

Why did the ant elope?
Nobody gnu.

What do you call a sick crocodile?
An illigator.

MICKEY MOUSE JOKE BOOK

© Disney

SILLY SPACEMEN

What do spacemen
call sausages?
Unidentified
Frying Objects.

Why did Mickey
Mouse take a trip
into outer space?
He wanted to
find Pluto.

Where do astronauts
leave their cars?
At parking meteors.

When do astronauts eat?
At launch time.

What do spacemen play in their spare time?
Astronauts and crosses.

How do you send a baby astronaut to sleep?
Rocket.

What did the alien say to the petrol pump?
"Take your finger out of your ear when I'm talking to you."

What do astronauts put in their sandwiches?
Launcheon meat.

WACKY WORLD

How did Vikings send secret messages to one another?
They used Norse code.

The trainee pilot was in trouble, so he radioed for help. "Mayday! Mayday!" he cried. The voice from the control tower calmly asked, "Please state your height and position." The pilot replied, "I'm five foot ten and sitting in the cockpit!"

How do people in Wales eat cheese?
Caerphilly.

Why is Europe like a frying pan?
Because it has Greece at the bottom.

Where do you always need to wear a coat?
In Chile.

In which country do people
have the biggest appetite?
Hungary.

Man: How much would it cost for you to
take me to the airport?
Taxi driver: £10.
Man: How much for my suitcase?
Taxi driver: No charge.
Man: Okay, then – you take my suitcase
and I'll walk.

Girl: I'm so glad I wasn't born in France.
Mother: Why's that?
Girl: Because I can't speak a word of French.

Son: Have you ever been to Egypt, Dad?
Father: No.
Son: Then where did you get Mummy?

FRUIT 'N' VEG

What is purple and hums?
An electric plum.

What sits in custard and looks cross?
Apple grumble.

What's green and hairy and wears sunglasses?
A gooseberry on holiday.

What do you give a sick lemon?
Lemonade.

What's purple and shouts "Help!"?
A damson in distress.

What comes out of the ground at ninety miles
an hour?
A turbo-charged carrot.

What do you do with a blue banana?
Try to cheer it up.

NIFTY NAMES

What do you call
a man who comes
through your
letter box?
Bill.

What do you call
a man who
loves fishing?
Rod.

What do you call a
man with a spade?
Doug.

What do you call
a man who's lost
his spade?
Douglas.

What do you call
a man who lives in
a bog?
Pete.

DOCTOR, DOCTOR!

Doctor, doctor! I feel like a pack of cards.
I'll deal with you later.

Doctor, doctor! I feel like an old sock.
Well, I'll be darned!

Doctor, doctor! Everyone keeps ignoring me.
Next, please.

Doctor, doctor! I feel like a spoon.
Sit still and don't stir!

Doctor, doctor! I can't sleep.
Sit on the edge of the bed and you'll soon drop off.

Doctor, doctor! I feel like an opera.
I must make some notes about your case.

Doctor, doctor! I feel like a bell.
Take this medicine, but if it doesn't help give me
a ring.

Doctor, doctor! I feel like a pair of curtains.
Pull yourself together!

Doctor, doctor! Can you help me out?
Which way did you come in?

Doctor, doctor! I keep thinking I'm an ant.
Stop bugging me!

Doctor, doctor! I've been stung by a bee!
I'll give you some cream to put on it.
Don't be silly, it'll be miles away by now.

SILLY SELECTION

What do you call a fish with no eyes? A fsh.

What's yellow, washable and never needs ironing? A drip-dry banana.

How do you get rid of a boomerang? Throw it down a one-way street.

Man in pet shop: Do you have any cats going cheap? Assistant: No, all our cats go meow.

Why don't bananas snore? They don't want to wake up the rest of the bunch.

What's the laziest mountain in the world? Mount Ever-rest.

Do tortoises have good memories?
Yes, they have turtle recall.

What do bees say
in hot weather?
"Swarm, isn't it?"

What did the earwig say
when it fell off a table?
"Earwigo!"

Who is the author of
Great Eggspectations?
Charles Chickens.

What do you get if cross a yeti
with a snail?
An Abominable Slow Man.

BRING ON BREAKTIME

What is everyone's favourite expression at school?
I don't know!

Teacher: Do you understand the importance of punctuation?
Pupil: Oh yes, I always get to school on time.

Headmaster: I hear you missed school yesterday.
Pupil: No, not one bit.

Mother: Did you enjoy your first day at school?
Daughter: First day? Do you mean I have to go back tomorrow?

Pupil: Excuse me, sir, but I don't think I deserve a mark of nought out of ten.
Teacher: Neither do I, but it's the lowest mark I can give.

Father: What are your marks like at school?
Son: They're underwater.
Father: What do you mean?
Son: They're below C level.

Teacher: Your essay about your cat is the same as your sister's.
Pupil: Yes, it's the same cat.

Teacher: What can you tell me about the Iron Age?
Pupil: Not much, I'm a bit rusty on that.

Teacher: What language do they speak in Cuba?
Pupil: Cubic?

Teacher: If I cut an apple into four pieces and a banana into eight, what will I get?
Pupil: Fruit salad?

WAITER, WAITER!

Waiter, waiter! This soup tastes funny.
Then why aren't you laughing?

Waiter, waiter! Have you got soup on the
menu today?
No, sir, I wiped it off.

Waiter, waiter! There's a fly in my soup.
Don't worry, sir, the spider in the salad
will get it.

Waiter, waiter! There's a little beetle
in my salad.
Sorry, sir, I'll fetch you a bigger one.

Waiter, waiter! I can't eat this meal – please
call the manager.
He won't want it either, sir.

Waiter, waiter! This coffee tastes like mud.
It was ground this morning.

Waiter, waiter! Will my beefburger be long?
I expect it'll be round, sir.

Waiter, waiter! What's this fly doing
in my soup?
Looks like the backstroke to me.

Waiter, waiter! How long will my spaghetti be?
I don't know, sir, I haven't measured it.

Waiter, waiter! I have a complaint.
This is a restaurant, sir, not a hospital!

BATTY BIRDS

What do you give a sick bird?
Tweetment.

Why do birds fly south for the winter?
Because it's too far to walk.

What's the difference between unlawful
and illegal?
Unlawful is against the law and illegal
is a sick bird.

What do you get if you cross a dog
with a chicken?
A hen that lays pooched eggs.

What kind of bird digs for coal?
A mynah bird.

Which bird always succeeds?
A budgie with no teeth.

What do you get when you cross a woodpecker
with a carrier pigeon?
A bird who knocks before delivering its message.

Which bird grows up while it grows down?
A duck.

What would you say to a miserable bird?
"Chirrup!"

Why do elephants paint
their toenails red?
So they can hide in cherry
trees without being seen.

Why do elephants wear green
felt hats?
So they can walk across snooker
tables without being noticed.

Why do elephants paint the
soles of their feet yellow?
So they can hide upside down
in a bowl of custard.

What's grey and has four
legs and a trunk?
A mouse going on holiday.

MICKEY MOUSE
JOKE BOOK

40

How can you tell when there's been an elephant in the fridge? There are footprints in the butter.

How do you get down from an elephant? You don't get down from an elephant, you get down from a duck.

How does an elephant get down from a tree? It sits on a leaf and waits for autumn.

What do get if you cross an elephant with a garden hose? A jumbo jet.

STUPID SWEETS

What's white and fluffy and swings through the cake shop?
A meringue-utan.

What cake flies through the air and comes back again?
A boomeringue.

What is pink, wobbly and flies?
A jellycopter.

How do jellies start their races?
Get set!

A rabbit raced a tortoise,
You know the tortoise won,
And Mr Rabbit came in late,
A little hot cross bun.

What is yellow and very dangerous?
Shark-infested custard.

What is yellow and a whizz at maths?
A banana with a calculator.

How can you make an apple puff?
Chase it round the garden.

Tim: Will you join me in an ice cream soda?
Kim: Okay, but you jump in first!

FUNNY FOOD

How do you stop meatballs from drowning?
Put them in gravy boats.

What's the main ingredient of dog biscuits?
Collie-flour.

When is rabbit stew horrible?
When it's got hares in it.

What do policemen eat in their sandwiches?
Truncheon meat.

What do motorcycle police eat in
their sandwiches?
Traffic jam.

What's a computer operator's favourite food?
Microchips.

What did the mayonnaise say to the refrigerator?
Shut the door, I'm dressing.

How do you make gold soup?
Put nine carrots in it.

What do you call two turnips in love?
Swedehearts.

What do you call a mischievous egg?
A practical yolker.

GHOSTLY GIGGLES

Why do witches ride broomsticks?
They can't afford vacuum cleaners.

How do you flatten a ghost?
Use a spirit level.

What do ghosts eat for lunch?
Ghoulash.

Who looks after spooks on an aeroplane?
Air ghostesses.

What do you call a play acted by ghosts?
A phantomime.

What did one ghost say to the other ghost?
Do you believe in people?

What should a short-sighted ghost have?
Spooktacles.

What haunts operating theatres?
Surgical spirits.

What do ghosts like to chew?
Boo-ble gum.

Where do ghosts like to go on holiday?
The Dead Sea.

MONSTER MADNESS

How does a monster try to do well?
He puts his beast foot forward.

Did you hear about the
monsters who got engaged?
It was love at first fright.

Which Scottish
monster is
always untidy?
The Loch Mess
Monster.

Did you hear
about the
monster who
only ate beans?
Human beans.

What do you do if a monster sits
in front of you in the cinema?
Miss the film.

What do monsters do
for a sore throat?
They gargoyle.